G000124092

contents

LARK CRAFTS

Published by Lark Crafts
An Imprint of Sterling Publishing Co., Inc.
387 Park Avenue South, New York, NY 10016

ISBN 978-1-4547-0022-7

This material originally appeared as part of *Pretty Little Mini Quilts* (ISBN 9781600594939). First publication in this format 2011.

© 2010, Lark Crafts

Distributed in Canada by Sterling Publishing,
c/o Canadian Manda Group, 165 Dufferin Street
Toronto, Ontario, Canada M6K 3H6

Distributed in the United Kingdom by GMC Distribution Services, Castle Place, 166 High Street, Lewes, East Sussex, England BN7 1XU

Distributed in Australia by Capricorn Link (Australia) Pty Ltd.,P.O. Box 704, Windsor, NSW 2756 Australia

Manufactured in China

Techniques

Putting together a quilt is just like putting together a sandwich. Take a look at figure 1: You put down your backing (the first slice of bread), then your batting (the filling), and cover it with your quilt top (the other slice of bread). No problem! Okay, maybe assembling a quilt is actually a little more complicated than slapping together a tuna salad on wheat. But reading the tips, tricks, and techniques in this section will give you the knowledge you need to create your own fabric masterpieces.

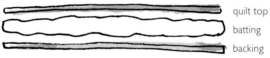

quilt top
batting
backing

figure 1

CUTTING

Let's back up a step for a second. Before taking scissors to fabric, your first move is usually to wash your fabrics, using the same settings you'd use when laundering the finished quilt. This will avoid any problems later with shrinkage or running colors. If your fabric gets super wrinkly in the wash, give it a quick pressing.

When it's time to cut your pieces to size, remember that you'll need to add about ¼ inch (6 mm) to each edge to accommodate the seam allowance, unless the instructions tell you not to add any allowance, or the materials list gives you an exact size to cut to. You can cut all your pieces before you start or cut them along the way, but be sure to keep your pieces organized and even labeled, if that helps avoid confusion.

A PERFECT CUT

When cutting with a rotary cutter and mat, follow these steps for a straight and safe cut. Hold the cutter at a 45° angle, with the blade firmly against the ruler's edge. Keep even pressure on the cutter, and always cut away from yourself. Keep the safety latch on when the cutter is not in use, and replace blades as needed.

MACHINE STITCHING

Unless you like to quilt when you're out and about (and have a lot of free time), most of the stitches in your mini quilts will probably be machine stitches. Before you begin, test the tension of your machine by stitching on a scrap of the fabric you'll be using. If necessary, follow the instructions in your machine's manual to adjust the tension for the top thread or the bobbin. Then follow these steps to sew the perfect seam.

1 Pin the fabric pieces together, using straight pins placed at right angles to the seam. Unless the project instructions tell you otherwise, most seams are sewn with right sides together and raw edges aligned.

2 As you sew, pull the pins out before they reach the needle. Be quick! If you're too late, the machine needle can nick the pins, which will dull or even break the needle.

3 To make a sharp angle for a corner, you need to pivot the fabric. When you get to the corner point, stop with the needle down in the fabric. Then lift the presser foot, turn the fabric, lower the presser foot, and keep on sewing.

4 Let the machine do the work of pulling the fabric through as you sew. This will save you uneven stitches, stretched fabric, puckered seams, and a lot of wasted energy.

5 Pay attention to those seam allowances, knowing that ¼ inch (6 mm) is pretty standard (figure 2). Use the measurement lines on the throat plate as a guide while you feed the fabric along.

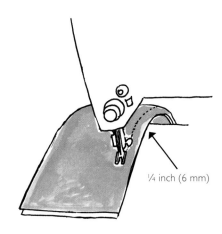

¼ inch (6 mm)

figure 2

basic quilting tool kit

- *Sharp sewing scissors (for fabric)*
- *Craft scissors (for paper)*
- *Sewing machine*
- *Sewing machine needles*
- *Hand-sewing needles*
- *Rotary cutter and mat*
- *Measuring tape*
- *Transparent ruler*

- *Tailor's chalk or water-soluble fabric marker*
- *Seam ripper*
- *Iron and ironing board*
- *Needle threader*
- *Straight pins*
- *Safety or basting pins*
- *Thread*
- *Pencil and paper for making templates*

PIECING

A few quilts in this book have one main piece for the quilt top, with decorative elements such as appliqué or embroidery added on top of it. Most quilts, though, require some amount of piecing, a process used in traditional quilts. True to its name, piecing involves small pieces being sewn together into larger units, and eventually into the entire quilt design.

A sewing machine is best for piecing, though piecing by hand is also possible. Here's how to do it.

1 Lay two pieces of fabric together with right sides facing.

2 Pin the pieces together along the edge where they will be joined.

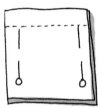

3 Straight stitch along the side, about ¼ inch (6 mm) in from the raw edge of the fabric (figure 3).

figure 3

4 Lay the pieces out flat, and, using an iron, press the seams to one side (making them lie under the darker fabric, if possible) or open, depending on the instructions (figure 4).

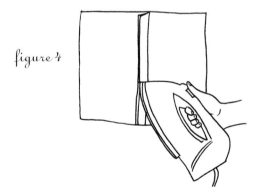

figure 4

ATTACHING A BORDER

Some quilts use borders to frame the central design. As in piecing, you'll attach a border using a ¼-inch (6 mm) seam allowance (unless directed otherwise) and then iron the seams to one side.

1 Cut fabric strips in the correct dimensions for each border of the quilt.

2 Working first on a short side of the quilt, pin the border strip to the quilt top with right sides together (figure 5).

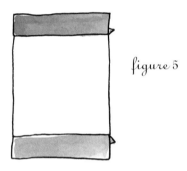

figure 5

3 Stitch along the edge, using a ¼-inch (6 mm) seam allowance. Press the seam out toward the border. Repeat steps 2 and 3 for the quilt's other short side, then for the two long sides (figure 6).

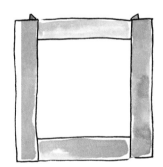

figure 6

BASTING

Your quilt top is cut, assembled, and embellished. Now it's finally time to start putting together that tasty quilt sandwich. Before you start sewing your layers together, you'll need to stack and baste the quilt top, batting, and backing to make sure they stay flat during the quilting process.

Iron your layers so they're smooth and free of wrinkles. Lay them out on a flat surface in the following order starting at the bottom: backing (face down), batting, and quilt top (face up). Make sure each layer is centered on top of the previous one. Starting in the center of the quilt and working out, pin, or baste, the layers together with safety or basting pins spaced about 6 inches (15.2 cm) apart (figure 7). When you've pinned your way around the quilt, check that all the layers are smooth and flat.

An important note: If you're finishing the edges using the quick turn method (where you stitch your layers together while inside out and then flip them right side out), you'll need to stack your layers in a different order before you baste them (see page 10).

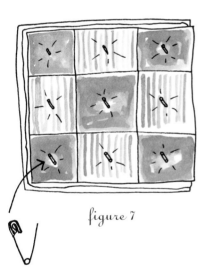

figure 7

QUILTING

Quilting is the part of the process that creates a padded, textured fabric, which is practical, decorative, and just plain fun to hold. Quilting can be done by hand or machine, but either way you should start by planning your stitch pattern. If you're doing something really complicated, you can draw out the pattern on your quilt top with chalk or a water-soluble fabric marker. The following techniques show you some of the many choices you have for making quilting patterns.

STRAIGHT-STITCH QUILTING

Straight-stitch quilting is the most basic type; it's the same type of stitch you used in piecing the quilt and other standard sewing tasks. If you're straight stitching by hand (also called a running stitch), keep your stitches short and even. For a clean finish, pull your knots through so they are hidden in the batting. On your machine, you might need to loosen the needle tension and lengthen the stitch to accommodate the thick layers. Even a mini quilt can have thick layers and some fairly large sections to keep out of the way as you sew; rolling up the edges can help you access the whole quilt as you go (figure 8).

figure 8

THE STRAIGHT TRUTH

Even a simple straight stitch has various options for giving your quilt a different look. "Stitch in the ditch" is a process that involves stitching along the seamlines of the quilt top's pieced sections, hiding your quilting stitches in the seams. You can also use the straight stitch to outline various design elements—such as appliqué or pieced shapes—to accentuate those details.

FREE-MOTION QUILTING

If you were the kind of kid who always colored with crayons outside the lines (and even if you weren't), free-motion quilting gives you complete control of the quilting stitch pattern, without any silly straight lines to worry about. For free-motion quilting on the machine, a darning foot—which has a circular opening for the needle to pass through—can help. You'll also need to disengage the automatic feed mechanism (usually called feed dogs). Control the movement of the fabric and the shape of the stitch by using two hands to spread the fabric out flat under the needle (figure 9). Guide the fabric to create any shape you like.

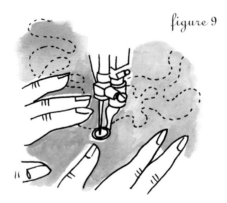

figure 9

TYING

Here's a technique that's quick and easy, and it can add some decorative interest to the front or back of your quilt. Tying involves connecting the quilt layers with a few stitches placed in a grid and tied. The knots can be placed on either side of the quilt. You can use embroidery floss, perle cotton, or yarn for this process (regular thread won't be thick enough). Here's how.

1 Check your batting for spacing suggestions, but 2 to 6 inches (5 to 15.2 cm) apart should be enough. You can use a ruler and chalk to mark a grid on your basted quilt top, or else place the ties randomly.

2 Thread a sharp hand-sewing needle with yarn (or whatever material you're using).

3 Stitch straight down through the quilt layers and then back up, making sure the layers don't shift as you work.

4 Tie the yarn tails in a knot. A square knot (figure 10) is easy to make and will stay firmly tied. Trim the ends to ¾ to 1 inch long (1.9 to 2.5 cm). Repeat steps 3 and 4 for each tie.

figure 10

BINDING

If a quilt top is the canvas, then binding is the picture frame. Besides adding a complementary or contrasting color to surround your mini quilt, binding is also darn useful for neatly holding the edges of your work together for years to come. The following sections give you several choices for finishing off your quilt.

MAKING YOUR OWN BINDING

You can buy premade binding at the fabric store, or you can make your own, in which case you'll have plenty of fabrics and widths to choose from. Rather than making binding pieces for each edge, it's usually easiest to make one very long length of binding and attach it around all the edges in one shot.

1 To determine the total length of the binding you'll need, add the lengths of the top, bottom, left, and right edges of the quilt, and add some extra length for safety.

2 Cut a strip following the recommended width in the pattern instructions.

3 If you need to connect strips together to make one long strip, one method is to pin and stitch the short ends together, with right sides facing, until you have one long strip, then press the seams open (figure 11).

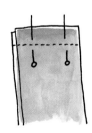

figure 11

4 A second method for connecting strips is to pin the short ends together at a right angle, with right sides facing, and stitch diagonally across the corner (figure 12). Trim the seam allowance and press the seams open.

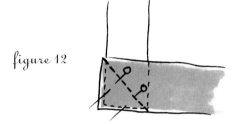

figure 12

SINGLE BINDING WITH MITERED CORNERS

Sometimes the instructions for a mini quilt will suggest a particular method, such as single-fold or double-fold binding, but it's really your call. (No one's checking up on you!) Single binding is one of the simpler methods you can use to finish a quilt.

1 After you've quilted the layers together, lay the quilt completely flat and trim the edges so the quilt top, batting, and backing are all the same size.

2 Starting midway on one edge or near a corner, pin and then stitch the right side of the batting to the right side of the fabric, folding over the starting edge (figure 13). Use the seam allowance in your instructions.

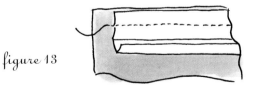

figure 13

3 Stop stitching as you approach the corner and clip the threads to remove the quilt from the machine. Fold the binding straight up over itself so a 45° angle forms at the corner (figure 14).

figure 14

4 Fold the binding straight down to make it even with the edge of the quilt and continue pinning and stitching the binding in place (figure 15). Continue working your way around the quilt, using the same process for the rest of the corners.

figure 15

5 When you near your starting point, stitch your binding strip over the folded-over starting edge of the binding strip. You don't need to fold back the raw edge at the very end of the binding strip—it'll soon be hidden.

6 Fold the binding strip over the edges (not too tightly) to the back of the quilt. Turn under the raw edge just enough to cover the seam that you just stitched. Place the prepared edge just barely over the seamline that attached the binding and pin it down along each edge. Create diagonal folds at each corner and then pin the corners in place.

7 Working from the top of the quilt, use a slipstitch by hand or stitch in the ditch to attach the binding to the back of the quilt (figure 16).

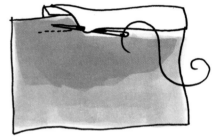
figure 16

BUTTED CORNERS

Butted corners may not look as neat as mitered corners (unless you think they do), but they do give you another choice when binding.

1 Working one edge at a time (instead of a continuous strip), pin and then stitch binding along the two short edges on the right side of the quilt.

2 Fold the binding to the back, tuck under the raw edge if the binding is single-fold, and then stitch it down on the back using the slipstitch or stitching in the ditch of the seam you just created.

3 Measure and then cut the length you'll need for the long edges of the quilt, adding a little extra to each end, and attach binding to the edges as you did with the short edges.

4 Turn under the extra binding at each end and use a slipstitch to secure the ends closed (figure 17).

figure 17

DOUBLE-LAYER BINDING

This method may be a little trickier, though the steps are essentially the same as in a single-layer binding. You will end with a mini quilt with a sturdier edge. Projects with double-layer binding usually tell you how wide to cut your strips, but in general, your strips will need to be about six times wider than the final binding width you're planning.

1 Following the instructions for your project, cut the strips and then sew them together.

2 Fold the binding strip in half lengthwise with wrong sides together and then pin it to the right side of the quilt top, lining up the raw edges. Work your way around the quilt using mitered or butted corners.

3 Stitch the binding in place using the recommended seam allowance, mitering the corners (or making butted corners if you wish) as you work around the quilt (figure 18).

figure 18

4 Fold the binding to the back of the quilt and then pin and stitch it in place. Since the fabric has been folded in half, you don't have to worry about turning under any raw edges (figure 19).

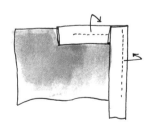

figure 19

QUICK TURNING A QUILT

Binding, schminding, you say? You want to avoid that step altogether, and not even have a border around your mini quilt? Then quick turning is the method for you. This process allows you to skip binding completely. It works particularly well if you plan on tying your quilt.

1 Stack your quilt by placing the batting on the bottom, followed by the backing, right side up, and the quilt top, centered with the right side down. Notice that this is different from the stacking described on page 5.

2 Pin the layers together along the edges, placing a few pins in the middle of the quilt to keep the layers smooth.

3 Stitch almost all the way around the outside edge of the quilt, using a ½-inch (1.3 cm) seam allowance. Leave about 10 inches (25.4 cm) unstitched for an opening to turn the quilt through.

4 Trim along the edges so all three layers are the same size, and cut across the corners to decrease bulk. Turn the quilt right side out and hand stitch the opening closed (figure 20).

figure 20

5 Baste the quilt using pins and then quilt, or tie, the layers.

HANGING A QUILT

Compared to regular quilts, mini quilts often spend a lot of their time just hanging around—up on the wall for everyone to admire. If your quilt has heavy interfacing or backing, you can add buttons or loops and a simple strand of yarn, elastic, or cord to create a hanger.

You can also consider adding a sleeve for a dowel rod or other hanging device. Cut a strip of fabric that's about 4 inches (10.2 cm) wide and almost as long as your quilt's width, turn and stitch under the short raw edges, and then pin and stitch the long edges together with right sides facing (figure 21). Turn the sleeve right side out and place it seam side down on the backing. Pin and hand stitch the sleeve in place along the top and bottom edges (figure 22). Slide a dowel rod, ribbon, or whatever you'd like through the sleeve, and you're ready to show off your newest masterpiece.

figure 21

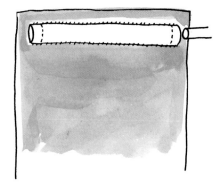

figure 22

center of attention

Capture the glory of autumn year-round with this beautiful and simple design.

DESIGNER

RUTH SINGER

WHAT YOU NEED

Basic Quilting Tool Kit (page 3)

Leaf templates

Circles (such as embroidery hoops) to draw circles around

Cream cotton, 32-inch (81.3 cm) square

Pink cotton, 32-inch (81.3 cm) square

Cotton batting, 32 inches (81.3 cm)

18 scraps of prewashed fabric in different materials and textures, about 4 inches (10.2 cm) square each

¼ yard (22.9 cm) lightweight iron-on interfacing

Coordinating fabric scraps to make about 4 yards (3.6 m) of binding strips

Variegated embroidery thread for quilting

SEAM ALLOWANCE

None

FINISHED SIZE

18¼ inches (46.4 cm) square

WHAT YOU DO

1 To prepare the 18 leaves, first iron interfacing onto the back of the fabric scraps. Trace a different leaf design onto each scrap and cut out.

2 Arrange 17 leaves in a circular design about 16 inches (40.6 cm) in diameter on the cream fabric and pin. Put the last leaf in the center. Hand stitch the leaves into place using a matching sewing thread, or a contrasting embroidery thread if you prefer.

3 Draw the quilting lines shown in the photo with a fabric marker, using embroidery hoops or plates to create the circles. The center circles are 4 inches (10.2 cm), 9 inches (22.9 cm), and 13 inches (33 cm) in diameter. The corner circles are 5 inches (12.7 cm) and 3 inches (7.6 cm) in diameter.

4 Layer the quilt with the pink backing face down, then the batting, then the quilt top facing up. Use safety pins or baste in place.

5 Hand quilt the circles through all layers in large running stitches, using the embroidery thread. Start at the innermost center circle and work out. You can start and fasten the thread between the backing and the batting.

6 Remove the pins or basting and trim the quilt down to 28 inches (71.1 cm) square, cutting close to the corner stitching.

7 To make the binding, cut strips 2½ inches (6.4 cm) wide in a range of different fabrics to match or coordinate with the leaves. Join together to make a total length of about 4 yards (3.6 m).

8 Bind the quilt by your preferred method.

TREE HUGGING

It only makes sense in a quilt design that celebrates the diversity of nature: Organic cotton was used here in the quilt top, the backing, and the batting.

checkered past

𝒴ou'll have plenty of squares to play with in this elegant geometric quilt.

DESIGNER

DORIE BLAISDELL SCHWARZ

WHAT YOU NEED

Basic Quilting Tool Kit (page 3)

Note: All fabric is 44 inches (1.1 m) wide.

¼ yard (22.9 cm) each of two red print cottons

¼ yard (22.9 cm) each of two gold print cottons

½ yard (45.7 cm) white cotton

¼ yard (22.9 cm) red cotton for the border

1 yard (.9 m) white cotton for backing

Low-loft cotton batting

¼ yard (22.9 cm) gold cotton for binding

SEAM ALLOWANCE

¼ inch (6 mm)

FINISHED SIZE

26½ x 32½ inches (67.3 x 82.5 cm)

WHAT YOU DO

1 From each of the two red and two gold fabric prints, cut five 1½-inch (3.8 cm) wide strips, each at least 15 to 16 inches (38.1 to 40.6 cm) long. Cut a total of 16 white strips of the same size. Also, cut 40 3½-inch (8.9 cm) squares from the white fabric.

2 For each of the red and gold prints, do the following. Sew three strips together in this pattern: color, white, color. Repeat the pattern with three more strips. Then sew three strips together as white, color, white. You'll have three strips of three, using a total of five color strips and four white strips. Press the seams toward the colored fabric. Cut each strip of three into 1½-inch (3.8 cm) segments.

3 Arrange three segments in a checkerboard pattern (figure 1). Stitch the segments together. Repeat this step until you have 10 checkerboard squares for each of the four colors.

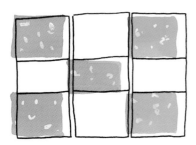

figure 1

4 Lay out the quilt as shown in the photo, alternating checkerboard squares with plain white squares.

5 Sew the top together: Make strips by sewing together all the squares in each horizontal row. Then sew the rows together, making sure to line up the seams between blocks.

6 Cut two 1½ x 24½-inch (3.8 x 62.2 cm) strips and two 1½ x 32½-inch (3.8 x 82.5 cm) strips from the solid red fabric. Add the border by first sewing the two shorter red strips to the shorter ends of the quilt, then sewing the remaining strips to the longer sides.

7 Make the quilt sandwich: Lay out the backing on a flat surface and smooth out any wrinkles. Lay the cotton batting on top, then cover with the quilt top. Smooth all the layers, and then baste them using safety pins.

8 Quilt the quilt using diagonal lines that run through all the large white squares and diagonal lines that run through all the checked squares. When you're done, each 3-inch (7.6 cm) unit will have an X through it.

9 Bind the quilt using the solid gold fabric and a ¼-inch (6 mm) binding (see pages 26–28 on binding techniques).

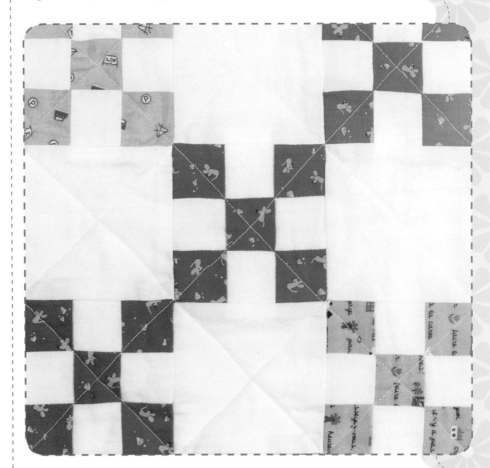

hearts on fire

DESIGNER

CINDY COOKSEY

$\mathcal{E}$ach of the hearts in this warm-toned quilt may differ in texture, color, and embellishment, but together they beat as one to make a beautiful design.

WHAT YOU NEED

Basic Quilting Tool Kit (page 3)

Background fabric, 18 x 16 inches (45.7 x 40.6 cm)

Low-loft batting, 18 x 16 inches (45.7 x 40.6 cm)

Cotton backing fabric, 18 x 16 inches (45.7 x 40.6 cm)

Contrasting thread for basting

16 scrap pieces of mostly red fabric for hearts, each at least 3 x 4 inches (7.6 x 10.2 cm)

Thin fusible web

Parchment paper or release paper to use with fabric fuse

Machine-quilting thread to match hearts

Perle cotton embroidery thread in a variety of weights in red, black, burgundy, and variegated

Metallic embroidery thread in silver and gold

Dark red metallic or similar fabric for binding, ¼ yard (22.9 cm)

Embellishments such as a red fabric-covered button, red beads (seed, bugle, and flat round), heart-shaped and other buttons or beads in red, metallic, or black

SEAM ALLOWANCE

None

FINISHED SIZE

14½ x 17 inches (36.8 x 43.2 cm)

WHAT YOU DO

1 Make a sandwich of the background fabric, batting, and cotton backing fabric. Pin together.

2 Baste around the outer edge. Then use a ruler and pins to locate a vertical line down the middle, and baste along the line. Use the same method to locate a horizontal line in the exact middle, and baste along that line. The basting lines will keep the silk background fabric from shifting around, and they will also help with placing the hearts.

3 Back most of the sixteen 3 x 4-inch (7.6 x 10.2 cm) fabric scraps with fusible web according to the manufacturer's instructions. Use release paper or parchment

SWEET HEARTS ARE MADE OF THIS

For the hearts, you can use a variety of silks, chiffon, velvet, lace, and sheers, with some solid and some printed or machine embroidered. Consider unexpected materials such as window screen and plastic "fishnet" material from a produce bag as well.

paper to protect surfaces from any melted fusible web. Some materials such as lace, window screen, and plastic fishnet will not be appropriate for fusing.

4 Trace a heart shape onto paper and cut out.

5 Pin the paper heart shape onto each fabric scrap and carefully cut out fabric hearts. There is no seam allowance.

6 Arrange the hearts on the prepared background fabric sandwich. Use the center horizontal and vertical lines to guide in placement: Place the tops of four hearts right along the horizontal line, with the bottom tips of the next row up also just touching the horizontal line. Center the hearts horizontally and place them about ½ inch (1.3 cm) apart vertically.

7 When you are happy with the arrangement, carefully iron down the hearts with fusible web on them, taking great care to keep the iron away from any window screen, plastic fishnet, or other materials that may be damaged by the heat. Pin the hearts without fusible web in place.

8 Some of the fused hearts can now be stitched down with free-motion machine quilting. Use thread that best goes with each heart—red in most cases. Stitch close to the edges, and stitch along the fabric design if desired. Leave some heart centers unquilted for later embellishment.

9 Use a hand blanket stitch around the edges of two or three of the fused hearts. Use contrasting embroidery thread such as black and metallic.

10 Use other hand embroidery to stitch down the edges of the unfused hearts, such as crisscross Xs and straight lines pointing inward.

11 Couch burgundy eyelash yarn around one heart (optional).

12 Using red perle cotton embroidery thread (red-to-burgundy hand-dyed if you can find it), hand embroider the

background fabric with random scattered stitches, about $^3/_8$ inch (9.5 mm) long. Make the stitches go in all directions. Continue the stitches to make a 1½-inch (3.8 cm) border on the background fabric, taking care not to extend stitches beyond this border.

13 Remove the basting thread, then trim the quilt with a rotary cutter, leaving a 1½-inch (3.8 cm) border around the hearts. This will make your quilt about 14½ inches (36.8 cm) wide and 17 inches (43.2 cm) tall.

14 Apply binding using your preferred method.

15 Embellish the centers of several hearts, but leave a few interesting ones unembellished to stand on their own. Suggestions for embellishing: Stitch a large button or charm in each upper center of several hearts. Use seed beads scattered randomly on one heart, and in snake patterns on another. Use bugle beads,

round flat beads, random-sized smaller red buttons, and other distinctive-looking beads, either scattered randomly or following the design on the fabric.

16 Use extra backing fabric to create a sleeve for hanging.

around the block

*T*his quilt is meant to have a random appearance, so be playful with your fabric selections. Try not to think too hard!

DESIGNER

REBEKA LAMBERT

WHAT YOU NEED

Basic Quilting Tool Kit (page 3)

Cotton fabric scraps in a variety of prints, each print in one of 5 colors: black, blue, green, yellow, and red

1½ yards (1.4 m) of 44-inch (1.1 m) wide white cotton for sashing and backing

2 cotton border pieces, 3 x 23 inches (7.6 x 58.4 cm)

2 cotton border pieces, 3 x 29 inches (7.6 x 73.6 cm)

Cotton batting

Pieced binding, 4 yards (3.6 m) long and 3 inches (7.6 cm) wide

SEAM ALLOWANCE

¼ inch (6 mm), unless otherwise noted

FINISHED SIZE

29 inches (73.6 cm) square

WHAT YOU DO

1 Cut nine sets of block pieces (A–E) in the following sizes.

- **A:** 2 x 3½ inches (5.1 x 8.9 cm)
- **B:** 2 x 3½ inches (5.1 x 8.9 cm)
- **C:** 1½ x 3½ inches (3.8 x 8.9 cm)
- **D:** 3 x 4½ inches (7.6 x 11.4 cm)
- **E:** 6 x 2 inches (15.2 x 5.1 cm)

Each of the five pieces within a block set should be a different color. Try to vary the colors of the pieces from set to set.

2 See the block assembly patterns on page 22. Piece each block according to one of the variations, using a ¼-inch (6 mm) seam allowance. No matter which variation, you start by sewing piece A to B along the long side. Then sew piece C to the AB. Next, sew D to ABC. Lastly, sew E to ABCD.

3 Once all the blocks are pieced, press and square them up by trimming the sides so that each block measures 6 x 6 inches (15.2 x 15.2 cm).

4 Cut the sash pieces from the white cotton in the following sizes, as shown in the sash assembly pattern on page 23.

- **aa:** 6 pieces, 2 x 6 inches (5.1 x 15.2 cm) each
- **bb:** 4 pieces, 2 x 20½ inches (5.1 x 52.1 cm) each
- **cc:** 2 pieces, 2 x 23½ inches (5.1 x 59.7 cm) each

5 Sew the sash pieces to the quilt blocks as shown in the sash assembly pattern on page 23. Begin by making three rows of blocks, with each row having three sewing blocks separated by two aa sash pieces.

6 Sew the three rows together by sewing bb sash + row 1 + bb sash + row 2 + bb sash + row 3 + bb sash. Sew the last two cc sash pieces to either side of the quilt top.

7 Sew the 23-inch (58.4 cm) border strips to the top and the bottom of the quilt top. Sew the 29-inch (73.6 cm) border strips to either side of the quilt top. Trim the border pieces as need to square up the top. Iron the quilt top.

8 Cut the quilt backing and batting a few inches larger than the finished quilt top. Make the quilt sandwich by layering the backing (right side down), the batting, then the quilt top (right side up). Baste the quilt together with safety pins or basting pins.

9 Quilt as desired, then trim the excess backing and batting.

10 Make your binding by sewing various 3-inch (7.6 cm) wide scraps together. After sewing the pieces end to end, fold the binding in half right sides together, then press.

11 Starting at the middle of one side of the quilt and using a ½-inch (1.3 cm) seam allowance, sew the binding to the right side of the quilt with the raw edges of the binding lined up with the raw edge of the quilt.

BLOCK ASSEMBLY PATTERNS

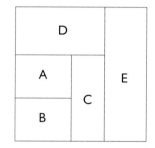

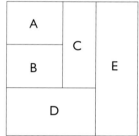

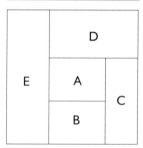

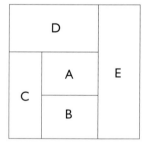

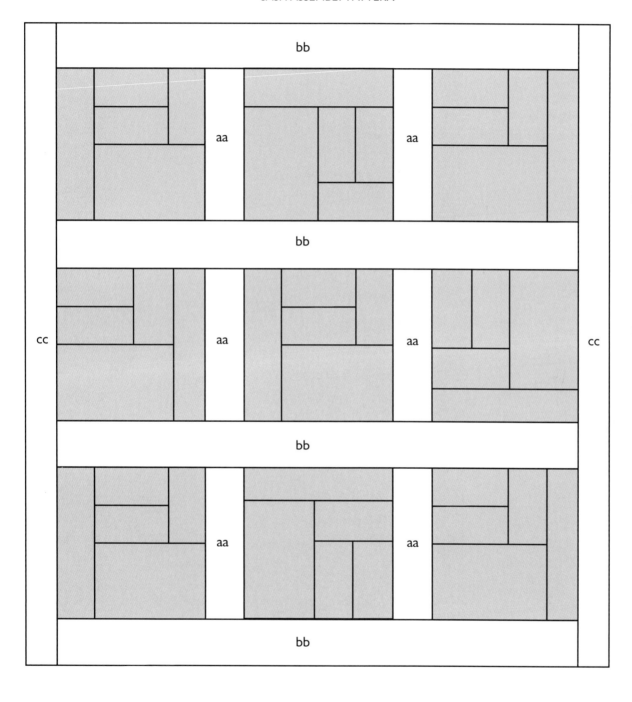

autumn breeze

DESIGNER

LOUISE PAPAS

After composing this seasonal scene, you may be inspired to gather fabrics in different tones to complete a series of quilts. Spring Mist or Summer Wind, anyone?

WHAT YOU NEED

Basic Quilting Tool Kit (page 3)

22 inches (55.9 cm) cream cotton, such as quilter's muslin or homespun

10 inches (25.4 cm) autumnal floral print cotton

Fat sixteenth (22.9 x 27.9 cm) of light brown patterned cotton

Fat sixteenth (22.9 x 27.9 cm) each of small-print yellow, red, brown, and orange cotton

Cream thread

23½ inches (59.7 cm) cotton in a coordinating color for backing

23½ inches (59.7 cm) cotton batting

Perle embroidery thread in cream

6 inches (15.2 cm) orange-and-cream-striped cotton fabric for binding

SEAM ALLOWANCE

¼ inch (6 mm)

FINISHED SIZE

19 x 20 inches (48.3 x 50.8 cm)

WHAT YOU DO

1   To make the quilt top, cut the cream fabric to 21 x 20 inches (53.3 x 50.8 cm). It will be cut to size before the binding goes on so that the edges are neat.

2   Draw a set of tree top, tree trunk, and leaf patterns onto tracing paper and cut these out for templates.

3   Pin the tree top and tree trunk templates onto the appropriate floral and light-brown fabrics and cut one of each. Take the leaf template and cut 26 leaves from a mixture of the red, orange, yellow, and brown fabrics.

4   Using the photo as a guide, place the tree trunk in position on the quilt top and pin. Appliqué the tree trunk onto the quilt top using the cream thread. Repeat with the tree top.

5   Using the photo as a guide, place the leaves on the quilt and pin them into position. Appliqué them onto the quilt top.

6   Cut the backing fabric and batting 1 inch (2.5 cm) larger than the quilt top. Place the backing right side down and place the batting on top. Then place the quilt top onto the batting right side up. Smooth it down so there are no wrinkles, and pin through all the layers with safety pins.

7   Using the perle thread, quilt ⅛ inch (3 mm) away from the edge of the tree top, tree trunk, and leaves.

8 Using a washable marker or pencil, mark up the branch and trunk details and wind swirls. Quilt these lines using the perle thread.

9 Trim the quilt to measure 19 inches (48.3 cm) wide and 20 inches (50.8 cm) high.

10 Bind the quilt with your preferred method, using the orange-and-cream fabric.

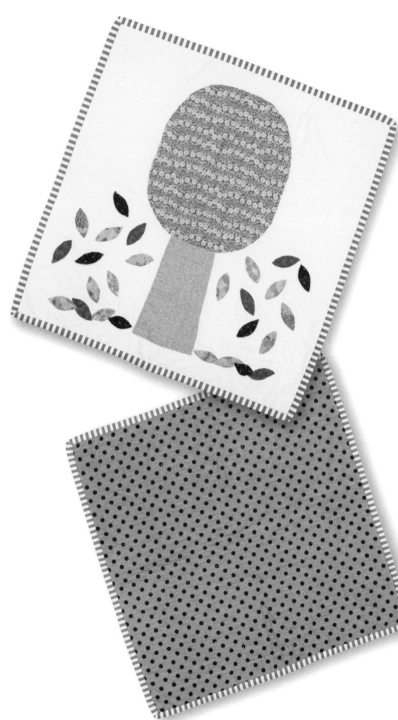

bright teeth

Two endless rows of triangles circle around delicate embroidery in this classic quilt.

WHAT YOU NEED

Basic Quilting Tool Kit (page 3)

¾ yard (68.6 cm) white cotton

Assorted fabrics in bright colors, enough for 28 squares, each 2⅜ inches (6.1 cm)

Green embroidery floss

Thin cotton batting, 23 x 18 inches (58.4 x 45.7 cm)

¼ yard (22.9 inches) green cotton for binding

SEAM ALLOWANCE

None

FINISHED SIZE

15 x 21 inches (38.1 x 53.3 cm)

DESIGNER

DORIE BLAISDELL SCHWARZ

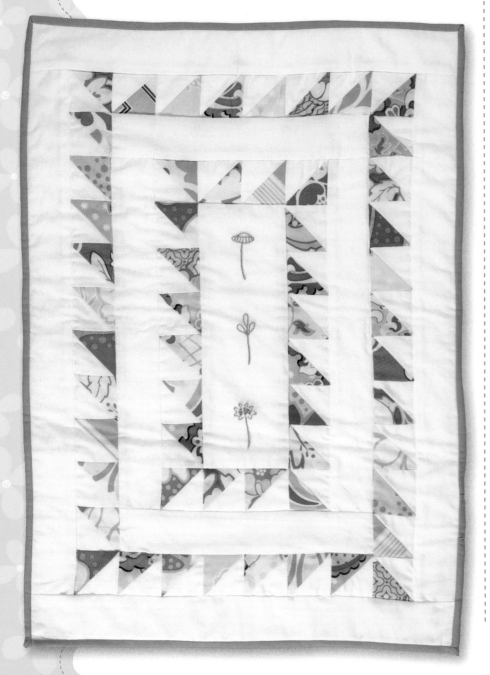

1 From the white cotton, cut the following pieces:

- One 23 x 18 inches (58.4 x 45.7 cm)

- 28 2⅜-inch (6.1 cm) squares

- One 9½ x 3½ inches (24.1 x 8.9 cm)

- Two 12½ x 2 inches (31.8 x 5.1 cm)

- Two 9½ x 2 inches (24.1 x 5.1 cm)

- Two 18½ x 2 inches (47 x 5.1 cm)

- Two 15½ x 2 inches (39.4 x 5.1 cm)

2 From the brightly colored fabrics, cut 28 2⅜-inch (6.1 cm) squares.

3 On the wrong side of each colored 2⅜-inch (6.1 cm) square, mark a line using a straight edge and pencil that goes diagonally across the square, from one point to its opposite point.

4 Bring together one white square and one colored square and line them up, right sides facing. Sew them together by sewing ¼ inch (6 mm) on each side of the diagonally drawn line. Repeat with the rest of the squares.

5 Cut the squares on the pencil line. Each sewn square becomes two half-square triangle units. Press the triangles open into squares, pressing the seams toward the colored fabric.

6 You now have all the pieces for the quilt top. Lay them all out so that they match the layout of the quilt in the photo. Pay careful attention to the direction of the triangle slant on each corner.

7 Starting with the rows around the center, sew the half-square triangles to each other, forming strips. You'll have two strips of six half-square triangle units, two strips of four half-square triangle units, two strips of ten half-square triangle units, and two strips of eight half-square triangle units.

8 Sew the six unit strips to the long sides of the 9½ x 3½-inch (24.1 x 8.9 cm) rectangle. Sew the four unit strips to the short side. Continue to build out from the center in this way. Next sew the 12½ x 2-inch (31.8 x 5.1 cm) white rectangles to the long side of the center, then add the 9½ x 2-inch (24.1 x 5.1 cm) white rectangles, and so on, until you have finished the top.

9 Embroider the motifs in the center using two strands of the green floss. The quilt shown here includes plant motifs with stem stitch for the stems, lazy daisy stitch for the lowest flower's petals, French knots for its center, and backstitch for the rest.

10 Make the quilt sandwich with white cotton on bottom, cotton batting in the middle, and the quilt top on top. Use safety pins to baste through all the layers.

11 Quilt the quilt by "stitching in the ditch"—stitch along all the seam lines of all the rectangles. Start in the middle and work your way out.

12 Bind the quilt using ¼-inch (6 mm) binding.

square deal

DESIGNER

MALKA DUBRAWSKY

*B*locks of bold color, squiggly lines, and delicate
French knots show that sometimes the simplest ideas are the best.

WHAT YOU NEED

Basic Quilting Tool Kit (page 3)

Template (page 62)

Note: All fabric is 44 inches
(1.1 m) wide.

¼ yard (22.9 cm) raspberry
cotton (piece 1)

¼ yard (22.9 cm) chartreuse
cotton (pieces 2, 5, and 6)

¼ yard (22.9 cm) kelly green
cotton (pieces 3 and 4)

⅛ yard (11.4 cm) raspberry-and-
orange-striped cotton (piece 7)

Embroidery hoop

Turquoise embroidery thread

Embroidery needle

½ yard (45.7 cm) cotton batting

½ yard (45.7 cm) teal cotton
for backing

Chartreuse thread

Machine-quilting thread in orange,
turquoise, and white

SEAM ALLOWANCE

¼ inch (6 mm)

FINISHED SIZE

18 x 23 inches (45.7 x 58.4 cm)

WHAT YOU DO

1 Use a copier to enlarge the
quilt template on page 62.
Cut apart the seven pieces.

2 Pin piece 1 to the raspberry
fabric and cut along the
edges adding the ¼ inch (6 mm)
seam allowance. Repeat with the
other six template pieces, pinning
them to their matching fabrics
and cutting.

3 Sew pieces 1 and 2 together
along their short edges.
Press the seam to one side. It's
best to alternate sides where
seams intersect.

4 Following the template
diagram, sew piece 3 to the
strip containing pieces 1 and 2
along its long edge. Press to one
side. Then sew pieces 4 and 5
together along their short edges.
Press to one side.

5 Sew the strip containing
pieces 4 and 5 to the strip
containing pieces 1, 2, and 3 along
the long edge. Press to one side.

6 Sew pieces 6 and 7 together
along their short edges. Press
to one side. Then sew the strip
containing pieces 6 and 7 to the
rest of the quilt top along the
long edge.

7 With a ruler and pencil, mark
the perimeter of the quilt
top to place French knots, with
knots about ½ inch (1.3 cm) from
each edge and spaced ½ inch
(1.3 cm) apart.

8 Place the quilt top in the
embroidery hoop and, using
turquoise embroidery thread,
stitch French knots where marked.
Reposition the embroidery hoop
as needed.

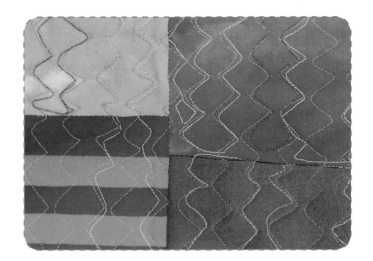

9 Lay the batting on your cutting mat, and lay the teal backing fabric right side up on the batting. Lay the quilt top right side down on the backing and batting. Pin the layers together and trim them even.

10 Sew the layers together, leaving a 9-inch (22.9 cm) gap along one side. Trim the corners. Turn the quilt right side out, making sure to poke out the corners.

11 Press the quilt flat and turn under a ¼-inch (6 mm) seam allowance at the gap. Pin. Using chartreuse thread and a hand-sewing needle, slip-stitch the gap closed.

12 Lay the quilt on the cutting mat and baste with safety pins about every 4 inches (10.2 cm). Free-motion machine-quilt with an allover squiggle pattern in orange thread, removing pins as you go. Accent some of the squiggles by machine-quilting in white and turquoise.

COMBINATION PLATE

Can't find a striped fabric you like for the corner of the quilt? You can make your own striped fabric by seaming together strips of 1-inch (2.5 cm) wide fabric in shades of raspberry and orange (or the colors of your choice).

portrait of Velma

You may think you're a quilter and not a portrait painter. Follow the simple techniques here and suddenly you're both.

DESIGNER

SUSAN LEWIS STOREY

WHAT YOU NEED

Basic Quilting Tool Kit (page 3)

Photograph

Computer with digital imaging software, or copy machine

Scanner and printer

Fabric treatment for making computer-printed fabrics washable

½ yard (45.7 cm) white cotton

½ yard (45.7 cm) contact paper

½ yard (45.7 cm) black cotton

Low-loft batting, 13 x 18 inches (33 x 45.7 cm)

Variegated quilting thread

Embellishments, such as buttons, beads, and decorative brads

Beading needle and thread

Embroidery thread and needle

SEAM ALLOWANCE

None

FINISHED SIZE

12 x 17 inches (30.5 x 43.2 cm)

WHAT YOU DO

1 Scan the photograph you're recreating with photo imaging software and resize the image to your desired dimensions. This portrait of Susan Lewis Storey's grandmother was resized to 12 x 17 inches (30.5 x 43.2 cm). Digitally correct any imperfections, and adjust the black-and-white balance of the photo. Add the outlines using a "posterization" filter to create the whimsical cartoon drawing effect.

2 To make the quilt without any digital imaging, start instead with this simpler photocopy method. Take the original photo to a local copy center, adjust the size and light/dark balance, print a black-and-white paper copy, color this by hand, and outline it as desired. Then scan that image into the computer before moving on to step 3.

3 Treat the white fabric with the fabric treatment according to its directions, air dry, and iron. Attach the treated white fabric to the contact paper, being careful to eliminate any wrinkling or bubbling. Cut the fabric and paper to the appropriate size for your printer.

4 Print the image onto the fabric. Remove the contact paper, then rinse, air dry, and iron the fabric.

5 Trim the black fabric to slightly larger than the batting. Layer the batting between the print and the black backing fabric. Using variegated thread, free-motion quilt the entire piece, then trim to size.

6 Cut 1 ½ yards (1.4 m) of black fabric strips 1 ½ inches (3.8 cm) wide for binding, and bind the quilt.

7 Embellish with a variety of beads, buttons, and embroidery to accent the image.

8 From the remaining black fabric, cut and attach a sleeve to the back for hanging.

SIZING IT UP

If you're able to use a large-format printer that will print up to the size of this quilt image—great! If you only have a standard printer, though, you can adjust the size of your project to suit your printer, or print opposite halves of your image on two separate sheets of fabric. Allow for a slight overlap on each print, then piece the halves together to create the size you want.

spring haiku

Colorful fabrics and some sweet embellishments make a lovely quilt.

Warm days and cool nights
Life begins its flow to roots.
Joy is in the air.

DESIGNER

KATHY DANIELS

WHAT YOU NEED

Basic Quilting Tool Kit (page 3)

¼ yard (22.9 cm) each of 5 or 6 different green cotton fabrics

¼ yard (22.9 cm) yellow cotton fabric

¼ yard (22.9 cm) varied cotton fabrics for flowers

½ yard (45.7 cm) fusible web

Fine-point marker

½ yard (45.7 cm) cotton batting

½ yard (45.7 cm) backing material

Yellow embroidery thread

Beads to embellish (your choice)

¼ yard (22.9 cm) black-and-white cotton fabric

SEAM ALLOWANCE

¼ inch (6 mm)

FINISHED SIZE

16 x 14 inches (40.6 x 35.6 cm)

WHAT YOU DO

1 Cut five strips of green fabric measuring 16½ inches (41.9 cm) long by varying widths to equal 8¼ inches (21 cm) when sewn together with ¼ inch (6 mm) seam allowances. Cut the yellow fabric to measure 16½ x 6¼ inches (41.9 x 15.9 cm). Strip-piece the greens together and sew them to the upper yellow piece. Press flat.

2 Choose your fabrics for flowers and stems, and iron fusible web to each back. Trace an oval pattern onto the paper backing of the fusible web, cut out two oval flower tops, and pin them to the right side of the yellow top. This will guide where to place your haiku.

3 Print out the words of the haiku shown here (or your own) from a computer, testing to find a font and size you like. Position your printed paper under the yellow background fabric and put it on top of a light box, tape it to a

window, or (if you can see the letters well enough) just leave it on the table. Trace it lightly in pencil and, when you're sure of the design, go over the letters with a fine-point marking pen to make it easier to see. This will be covered with thread.

4 Assemble your quilt sandwich—quilt top, batting, backing—and baste well. Use a dark thread to begin machine quilting your letters one at a time. Go very slowly, cutting threads as you go. Go over each letter about three times before moving on to the next. Hint: If this seems difficult to you, try a practice piece first.

5 When the script is done, quilt the lower section very simply by using a running stitch along the seams.

6 Cut out your flowers and stems freehand and position them to your liking. Iron them in place. Stitch with coordinating

thread colors around the flowers, leaves, and stems. The ferns were stitched using a free-motion zig-zag, but you could also do them with a regular machine zigzag.

7 Use a pencil to lightly sketch some lines to represent air currents through the yellow background. Hand-quilt these lines with two strands of yellow embroidery floss.

8 Embellish the edges of the oval flowers by using a but-tonhole stitch to apply medium-sized beads. Embellish with small beads on the tops of the other flowers and anywhere else you like.

9 Bind the edges with the black-and-white fabric. If you wish, use the same fabric to sew a sleeve onto the top of the back of the quilt for hanging.

have a cup

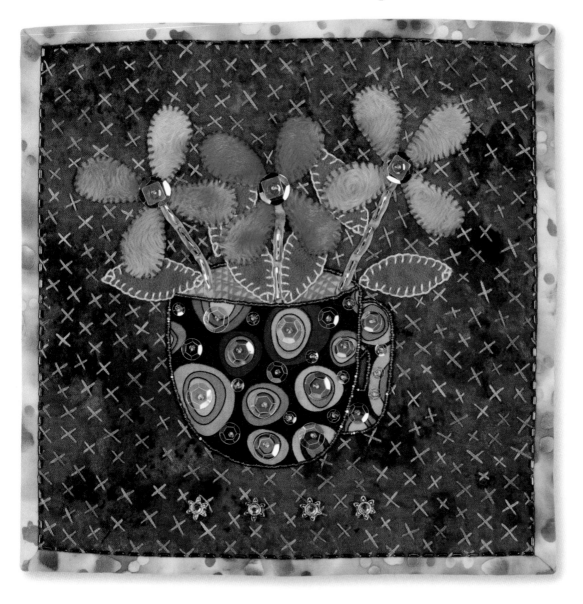

DESIGNER

MARY HUBBARD

*D*o you know someone who loves to sip tea out in the garden? Have we got a quilt to make for her!

WHAT YOU NEED

Basic Quilting Tool Kit (page 3)

1 sheet quilt of template plastic at least 5 x 5 inches (12.7 x 12.7 cm)

Silver quilt-marking pencil

⅛ yard (11.4 cm) cotton print for teacup

⅛ yard (11.4 cm) blue cotton for inside of cup

⅛ yard (11.4 cm) synthetic fur in pink/red for petals

⅛ yard (11.4 cm) green polyester or wool felt for leaves

1 fat quarter of cotton for background

Embroidery, chenille, quilt basting, and beading needles

Yellow and red perle cotton

Light green silk embroidery ribbon, 4 mm wide

1 fat quarter of cotton for backing

1 fat quarter of cotton batting

1 full skein of variegated blue-green embroidery floss

⅛ yard (11.4 cm) cotton fabric for binding

White beading thread

Twisted silver-lined bugle beads in chartreuse, size 5

About 32 sequins in different colors and varieties, including clear rainbow and metallic

Seed beads in cranberry luster, size 11

Metallic iris bugle beads in brown, size 1

Charlotte beads in purple iris AB, size 13

SEAM ALLOWANCE

Varies

FINISHED SIZE

8⅜ inches (21.3 cm) square

WHAT YOU DO

1 Use a pencil to draw or trace pattern pieces onto the plastic template sheet for the following: cup, cup handle, inside of cup, petal, and leaf. Cut out the templates. Using the templates and the silver quilt pencil, trace the cup, cup handle, and the inside of the cup on the right side of your chosen fabrics and cut out with a ¼-inch (6 mm) seam allowance around each piece. Next, trace the 12 flower petals and six leaves on the wrong side of your chosen fabrics and cut out on the drawn line.

2 Cut a square of background fabric 8½ x 8½ inches (21.6 x 21.6 cm). Using a light box or a bright window and the silver marking pencil, trace the cup, cup handle, and the inside of the cup on the fabric.

3 With matching cotton sewing thread and an appliqué needle, appliqué the inside of the teacup piece in place. Needle-turn appliqué is always worked from

right to left. Bring your needle up from the back of the block at the corner of the pattern drawn on your blue fabric. Use your needle to gently sweep a small section of the seam allowance under along the drawn line. Insert the needle straight down into the background fabric right next to the fold of your blue fabric. Taking a small stitch, bring the needle back to the front on the fold once again, catching a few threads of the blue fabric. You don't need to appliqué the bottom of the pattern because that will be covered when you appliqué the teacup in place.

4 Align the cup handle and pin in place. Appliqué the cup handle in place. To appliqué the inside curve of the handle, you'll need to clip an upside down Y-shape in the center of the seam allowance. Needle-turn appliqué the inside curve as before, using very tiny stitches and sweeping the seam allowance under with your needle. You don't need to appliqué the ends of the handle as they will be covered when you appliqué the teacup in place.

5 Position the teacup and pin in place. Appliqué the teacup in place as you did the cup inside and handle.

6 Position the leaves in place and pin. Embroider them to the background with an embroidery needle and yellow perle cotton, using a buttonhole embroidery stitch.

7 Position the flower petals and pin. Using the embroidery needle and the red perle cotton, attach the flower petals with a straight stitch similar to appliqué but working farther into the petal fabric.

8 To sew the flower stems, cut a piece of light emerald green silk ribbon embroidery ribbon 4 or 5 inches (10.2 or 12.7 cm) long for each stem. Using a chenille needle, take one long straight stitch starting at the lip of the cup and ending in the center of the flower.

9 Cut a 10 x 10-inch (25.4 x 25.4 cm) square of backing fabric and cotton batting. Layer the backing, batting, and quilt top and baste all three layers with cotton thread and a quilt-basting needle.

10 Using three strands of variegated embroidery floss and an embroidery needle, embroider the entire background of the quilt all the way to the edges of the quilt top with X's. The stitches should be randomly placed and vary slightly in size. Remove the basting stitches. Trim the excess batting and backing from the quilt so that it measures 8⅜ inches (21.3 cm) square.

11 Cut a straight strip of binding 2 inches x 44 inches (5.1 x 111.8 cm) from the binding fabric. Lay the strip horizontally with the wrong side facing up. Working with the left end of the strip, make a triangle fold, bringing the lower left corner up to meet the top raw edge of the strip and press. Clip excess fabric in the fold so that it's a generous ¼-inch (6 mm) seam allowance. Refold, and press the entire strip in half lengthwise.

12 Pin the binding in place, matching raw edges. Begin stitching about ½ inch (1.3 cm) below the angled fold and stop ¼ inch (6 mm) from the bottom edge of the quilt, using a ¼-inch (6 mm) seam allowance. Back tack at the beginning and the end of the stitching.

13 To form the mitered corner, first remove the quilt from the machine. Fold the binding strip at a 90-degree angle so that the raw edge of the binding and the raw edge of the next side of the quilt form a straight line. Fold the binding back along the quilt, matching raw edges, and pin. Begin stitching ¼ inch (6 mm) from the top and stop ¼ inch (6 mm) from the bottom. Back tack at the beginning and the end of the stitching. Work each corner in this manner. When you begin the last side, trim the excess binding at an angle so that it will gently slide inside the angled fold at the beginning of the binding. Pin in place, and beginning ¼ inch (6 mm) from the top edge, stitch this last side, stitching about 1 inch (2.5 cm) past the joint in the binding. Back tack the beginning and the end of the stitching.

14 Beading the quilt is done before you turn the binding with white beading thread and a beading needle. Beginning with the flower stems and using the chartreuse bugle beads, position the ribbon into the curve you want for the stem. While holding it in place, bring the beading needle up from the back of the quilt. Add one green bugle bead. With the bead laying flat against the ribbon, insert the needle back into the ribbon at the very end of the bead. Leave a small space and come up again, adding another bead and repeating the stitch.

15 To bead the flower centers, bring the needle up in the center of the flower. Add one large sequin, one medium square sequin, one round sequin and one cranberry seed bead. Skipping the cranberry bead, return needle back through all three sequins and back into the quilt. Go through each sequin and bead again, returning in the same manner and skipping the cranberry bead. This will secure the sequins and make the bead stand up with the side of the bead facing out.

16 Sew three sizes of clear rainbow sequins randomly over the surface of the teacup. Bring the needle up from the back and add a sequin followed by one cranberry seed bead. Skipping the seed bead as before, insert the needle back through the sequin. Repeat, skipping the seed bead again to secure the sequin.

17 Outline the entire teacup and handle with purple charlotte beads, using beading thread and the beading needle. Add five beads at a time, inserting the needle back into the quilt at the end of the line of beads and back up between beads 2 and 3 and through beads 3, 4, and 5 again. This keeps the beads close to the fabric and makes the next beads added fit snugly up against the first set with no gaps.

18 Outline the quilt with the brown bugle beads sewn right next to the binding.

19 Turn the quilt binding to the back and tack down with an appliqué stitch, using matching cotton thread and the appliqué needle. When you are finished turning the binding, stitch the fold where you joined the two ends of the binding closed.

hop in your step

Υou can never be too old (or young) to enjoy seeing a simple and charming scene hanging on the bedroom wall.

WHAT YOU NEED

Basic Quilting Tool Kit (page 3)

Light green cotton, one piece 8 x 3 inches (20.3 x 7.6 cm) and one piece 7 x 3 inches (17.8 x 7.6 cm)

Dark green cotton in these sizes: 10 x 2½ inches (25.4 x 6.4 cm), 12 x 2½ inches (30.5 x 6.4 cm), and 8 x 2½ inches (20.3 x 6.4 cm)

White cotton, one piece 7 x 9 inches (17.8 x 22.9 cm) and one piece 9½ x 12 inches (22.9 x 30.5 cm)

Embroidery floss in light green, dark green, brown, light brown, cream, and white

Batting, 9½ x 12 inches (24.1 x 30.5 cm)

Green bias tape, two 11-inch (27.9 cm) and two 14-inch (35.6 cm) pieces

SEAM ALLOWANCE

¼ inch (6 mm)

FINISHED SIZE

9½ x 12 inches (24.1 x 30.5 cm)

WHAT YOU DO

1 To make the front quilt piece, sew together the two light green and three dark green piece with the 7 x 9 inch (17.8 x 22.9 cm) white piece as shown in the photo. You'll need to cut a curve along the top of the shorter light green piece to make the hilltop.

2 Draw lines for the embroidery pattern with a fabric marker onto the quilt front and embroider the design with the floss.

3 Sandwich the quilt front, batting, and remaining 9½ x 12-inch (22.9 x 30.5 cm) white piece together and pin with safety pins, starting in the center. Quilt the layers together using the tying method, with bits of embroidery floss to match the fabric colors on the front. Make the knots at the back.

4 Sew the bias tape around the edge, folding in the corners.

spanish flowers

DESIGNER

CINDY COOKSEY

*T*he hexagons in this geometric quilt allow you to create what seems like 50 *really* little mini quilts, each with its own unique combination of fabric, stitching, and embellishment.

WHAT YOU NEED

Basic Quilting Tool Kit (page 3)

Sheets of paper hexagon templates, with each side of the hexagon 1 inch (2.5 cm) long

25 pieces of cotton fabric, each at least 3 x 6 inches (7.6 x 15.2 cm), in red, magenta, orange, yellow, green, blue green, blue, and purple

Batting, 13 x 15 inches (33 x 38.1 cm)

Cotton fabric for backing, 13 x 15 inches (33 x 38.1 cm)

Beads, buttons, and other embellishments (such as shisha mirrors)

SEAM ALLOWANCE

¼ inch (6 mm)

FINISHED SIZE

12 x 14 inches (30.5 x 35.6 cm)

WHAT YOU DO

1 Cut out 50 paper hexagon templates. (Note: You can create printable hexagon templates in any size you choose for free at online sites such as www.incompetech.com/graphpaper/hexagonal.) Pin a template on the wrong side of one of your 25 fabric pieces, leaving room to put another template on the other half of the piece. Cut the fabric around the template, leaving a ¼ inch (6 mm) seam allowance. Repeat until you have created 50 fabric hexagons (two from each fabric piece), each pinned with a template (figure 1).

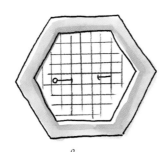

figure 1

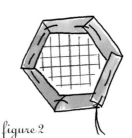

figure 2

2 For each hexagon, turn over the seam allowance on each edge, and baste the seam allowances down (figure 2).

3 Start arranging the 50 hexagons in a pleasing pattern, leaving open spaces as in the quilt pictured here. To begin sewing the hexagons together, place two of them right sides together. Whipstitch one edge down, using tiny stitches in a matching thread so they won't be too noticeable. Try to avoid sewing into the paper templates. Knot at the end of the edge and cut the thread. Open the hexagons out to show two side-by-side hexagons.

4 Place another hexagon onto one of the attached hexagons, right sides together, and whipstitch as before. Continue until you have completed the top row of six hexagons. Keep the paper templates attached to the hexagons until instructed to remove them.

5 Make the second row of hexagons the same as the first, except with seven hexagons. Continue making rows of hexagons, alternating six or seven in each row, until you have five rows. Referring to the photo of the quilt, sew together shorter rows of two or three hexagons to allow for the gaps in between.

6 Begin sewing the rows to each other, starting with the top two rows. As before, place right sides together, one edge at a time, securing the corners with an extra stitch or two. You'll need to fold adjacent hexagons out of the way as you sew each edge. After

you've sewn all the rows together as in the quilt photo, press them with an iron on a cotton setting. Carefully remove the basting threads and then all the paper hexagon templates. (They can be used again for other projects.) Keep the seam allowances folded in place.

7 Pin the batting to the back of the quilt top, with pins on the right side of the quilt top. Use one pin in each of the outer hexagons and at least some of the inner hexagons. Carefully cut the batting to exactly the same shape as the top, following the angles of each hexagon and cutting out the three holes with no hexagons.

8 Pin the backing fabric to the back of the quilt, with the right side facing out. As you place new pins into the quilt sandwich, you may remove the old pins that had secured the batting. Carefully cut the backing as you did the batting.

9 Fold the seam allowance of the backing so that it folds over the batting edge and the seam allowance slips between the batting and the quilt top. You'll need to clip the seam allowance of the backing fabric at the inner corners, taking care not to clip too far in. Blind-stitch the backing fabric to the quilt top, securing the inner and outer corners with an extra stitch or two. Use the same process to finish the three holes.

10 Remove the pins. Quilt each hexagon shape as desired. This quilt uses a spiral quilting design for most hexagons, with some having spokes in a starburst design.

11 Embellish the center of each hexagon with beads, buttons, or shisha mirrors.

12 Prepare for hanging by adding a standard quilt sleeve on the top half of the backing, using the remaining fabric of your choice.

DASH TO YOUR STASH

Think of this quilt as a chance to use just about any embellishment in your collection—from seed, bugle, ladybug, and butterfly beads to heart, flower, and leaf buttons. The tiny round shisha mirror included (see the middle of the detail photo below) is an example of an Indian embroidery technique that originally used pieces of mica to add shiny reflections to fabric work.

shrine to pretty little things

If you're reading this book, you must like things that are pretty and little. Now it's time to show how much you really care.

DESIGNER

JAMIE FINGAL

WHAT YOU NEED

Basic Quilting Tool Kit (page 3)

1 yard (.9 m) fabric for background

1 ½ yards (1.4 m) fabric for border and backing

¼ yard (22.9 cm) fabric with a wood print

¼ yard (22.9 cm) black fabric for outline of shrine

¼ yard (22.9 cm) fabric for background in shrine

Fusible web

Graph paper

Parchment paper

1 yard (.9 m) wool felt or a blend of rayon and wool

Embellishments, such as a zipper, mini safety pins, a mini belt buckle, a cloth measuring tape, silver snaps and buttons, mini pearl beads, a doll purse and shoes, a crown charm, and lace

Black embroidery thread

Waxed bead thread

Embroidery needle

Small needle for beading

Fabric glue

SEAM ALLOWANCE

None

FINISHED SIZE

16¼ x 21½ inches
(41.3 x 54.6 cm)

WHAT YOU DO

1 Choose contrasting fabrics for the interior of the shrine and the background. You want the colors to pop when they are together.

2 Iron all your fabrics onto the fusible web. Draw your design for the shrine on graph paper.

3 Start building your shrine. Lay the pattern onto the wood fabric and pin it into place. Cut it out along the outer edge.

4 Lay the wood-fabric shrine onto parchment paper (to protect your iron) and iron into place. Cut ¼-inch (6 mm) strips of the black fabric to use as an outline for the shrine. Lift up the outer edges of the shrine carefully and lay the strips underneath, ironing them into place as you go. Continue all the way around.

5 Cut the three pieces of fabric for the interior of the shrine as follows: a triangle with a base 5½ inches (14 cm) wide and sides measuring 3⅞ inches (9.8 cm) each for the roof; a rectangle, 4¾ x 5½ inches (12 x 14 cm) for the middle; and a rectangular strip for the lower section, 6¾ x 2¼ inches (17.1 x 5.7 cm). Center the pieces on the appropriate parts of the shrine, making sure the middle section is about 1 inch (2.5 cm) from the shrine sides. Iron into place.

6 With the ¼-inch (6 mm) strips that you have left over, outline the triangle top interior section and the bottom section. Use two strips to divide the latter into three square openings.

7 Lay the background fabric (the blue fabric in the photo) on top of the felt, making sure that it reaches about 1 to 2 inches (2.5 to 5.1 cm) from the edges of the felt. Iron it down so that it is flat and smooth.

8 Remove the shrine from the parchment paper and place it on top of the background fabric. Center it into place and iron it down.

9 Pin down the measuring tape around the center interior section of the shrine, leaving about ½ inch (1.3 cm) of wood fabric on the sides. Take apart the zipper and cut it to fit into place, under the inside portion of the measuring tape, and re-pin it. With a zipper foot on your sewing machine, sew the zipper into place along the inside edge of the measuring tape. Then, with your regular foot and black thread, sew the zigzag stitch on the outer edges of the measuring tape.

10 Cut out the dress, and iron it on in the middle of the middle interior rectangle. Then sew it into place using a free-motion foot.

11 Sew the entire shrine onto the background with black thread, using the zigzag stitch with a free-motion foot. Then change the stitch to straight, and free-motion the wood patterns in the shrine fabric to add texture to your piece.

12 Change the thread to match the background, and free-motion machine-quilt it down.

13 Cut four pieces of fabric, each about 5 inches (12.7 cm) wide, for the border. Make the curved edge by trimming the fabric strips on one side, cutting around the flowers in the fabric pattern.

14 Place the border fabric on each side so it extends about 2 to 3½ inches (5.1 to 8.9 cm) into the center. The remainder of the border strip will wrap around the edge of the quilt to the back. Begin ironing down the border one side at a time, flipping the quilt over to iron the fabric to the back. Clip excess fabric in the corners if needed. You will secure this into place later.

15 Begin attaching the embellishments. For the mini pearls on the dress, hand sew using a beading needle and waxed bead thread. Sew the pearls on one at a time with a double thread, knotting it on the back of the piece.

16 Sew the buttons on one of the three openings in the bottom section of the shrine, using perle cotton thread, going through each hole twice and knotting on the back to secure. Hand sew on the lace in the middle portion. You can glue smaller embellishments into place with the adhesive, applying it with a toothpick and letting it dry 24 hours, before you go back and sew them into place. Sew the medium silver snaps onto the four corners of the center section of the shrine.

17 Glue and sew the doll accessories into place on the top portion, along with the crown. Using one of your tiny buttons, sew black thread through it twice and knot it, then place it with a drop of glue onto the purse.

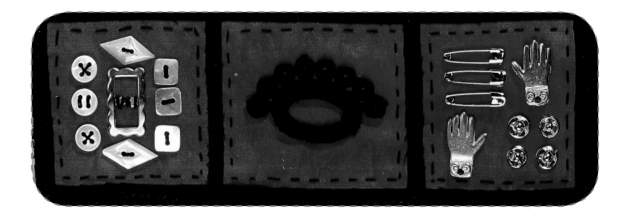

18 Using the black embroidery thread, sew a running stitch just inside the interior pieces of fabric on the shrine.

19 For the backing, place your quilt face down on an ironing surface. Cut the backing to cover the felt, which should be about ¾ to 1 inch (1.9 to 2.5 cm) from the sides. Iron it on carefully, so as not to disturb the embellishments on the front.

20 With black thread in your machine, sew around the outer portion of the shrine. Then change your thread to match the border fabric color and free-motion machine-quilt the entire border.

FUSE OR LOSE

Fusible web is truly one of the sewing world's great inventions. In this project, the entire piece has been fused to black wool felt. Each section was fused individually and the backing was fused on as well.

the elusive batiki bird

You say you've never even heard of a batiki bird before?
Now that you've spotted one, it's time to make your own.

DESIGNER

SARAH ANN SMITH

WHAT YOU NEED

Basic Quilting Tool Kit (page 3)

4 pieces of white-on-white print, each 7 x 30 inches (17.8 x 76.2 cm)

1 piece of pale green-gray fabric, 5 x 30 inches (12.7 x 76.2 cm)

14 to 16 pieces of blue, teal, and green batiks, 2½ to 4 inches (6.4 to 10.2 cm) wide by 7 inches (17.8 cm) long

Fusible web, 9 x 12 inches (22.9 x 30.5 cm)

Hot pink/orange batik, 9 x 12 inches (22.9 x 30.5 cm)

Variegated embroidery floss in magenta/pink and orange/yellow

Embroidery needle and hoop

Cotton fabric for backing, 30 inches (76.2 cm) square

Cotton batting, 29 inches (73.6 cm) square

Quilting thread in complementary colors

½ yard (45.7 cm) batik or near solid for binding

SEAM ALLOWANCE

¼ inch (6 mm)

FINISHED SIZE

26½ inches (67.3 cm) square

WHAT YOU DO

CUTTING AND PIECING

1 To make the background, cut each white-on-white fabric into four long wedges; one wedge should be about 3½ inches (8.9 cm) on the wide end. Cut the remaining section into three pieces with the narrowest end no smaller than 1 inch (2.5 cm) wide.

2 Cut the pale green-gray fabric into three long wedges with the narrow end no narrower than about 1 inch (2.5 cm).

3 Lay out your strips, alternating fabrics. Turn so that approximately every other one the wide end of the wedge is at the top. Using a washable marking pen or pencil, number your strips at the very bottom from left to right so the order doesn't get confused while stitching.

4 Machine-piece six to eight strips to make the section to the left of the tree trunk about 8 to 9 inches (20.3 to 22.9 cm) wide. Machine-piece the remaining strips for the section to the right of the tree trunk. Press all seam allowances toward the tree trunk.

5 To make the tree trunk and branches, cut each small chunk of the blues, teals, and greens into two wedges. As you did with the background, alternate the wide end of the strips to create a stack of "logs" 30 to 32 inches (76.2 to 81.3 cm) long. Trim the edges and cut your tree trunk to be 3½ inches (8.9 cm) wide at the bottom and 2½ inches (6.4 cm) wide at the top.

6 Cut the remaining piece of fabric into two narrower strips, at least 1 inch (2.5 cm) wide on the narrow end, to use for the branches. Press all seam allowances in one direction.

> ### INSTANT VARIETY
>
> If you don't have an extensive stash, look for some fat quarters that have a lot of color variation in them, then "swiss cheese" cut chunks from various parts of the fat quarter to make it look like they were cut from different fabrics.

7 To piece the background to the tree, place your tree trunk so that it overlaps the two background pieces. Cut the background pieces along the edges of the tree trunk. Place the remaining two narrower strips of tree as branches. Divide the long strip on the left and use the remainder for the small upper branch on the right.

8 Using a washable marking pencil or pen, mark the outside edge of your branches. Remove the branch, then mark ½ inch (1.3 cm) inside this line. These inner (pink) lines will be your cutting lines (and not the outside line).

9 Piece your background as shown in the photo in this order. Sew the left branch to the upper and lower background pieces. Sew the small upper branch on the right to the small triangle of background and the center background section. Sew the larger branch on the right to the upper and lower portions of the background. Press the seams toward the branches so that the branches appear to be in front of the background.

CREATING THE APPLIQUÉ BIRD

10 Apply fusible web to the back of your bird fabric. Mark the outline of the bird (by copying the bird here or creating your own) and cut out. Position your bird using the quilt photo as a guide and fuse in place.

11 You can embroider the bird now or after you have quilted this piece. If you wait until later, the back of your embroidery stitches will show on the back of your quilt. You can embroider as you wish: The quilt pictured here uses strands of pink variegated and yellow-orange floss in different combinations, with a feather stitch for outlining and a straight stitch elsewhere. Whether you embroider before or after quilting, a hoop will keep the top flat as you stitch.

12 When the top is done, press and trim to 28 x 28 inches (71.1 x 71.1 cm). Make sure the overall impression of the background piecing and tree trunk is vertical, not tilted.

A PAINTER'S LIGHT

You can create a subtle sense of space by selecting light and dark shades of the same color for your quilting and arranging them to make it appear the light is coming from one direction. For example, the tree trunk here uses a medium-dark blue on the left side for the contour lines, and a brighter aqua on the right side, the side of the light source.

LAYERING AND QUILTING

13 Place your backing fabric face up on the table, then the batting, and finally your neatly pressed top. Baste using your favorite method.

14 Hand- or machine-quilt the piece. First, quilt in the ditch (on the background side of the piecing lines, right next to the seam line) around the tree trunk and branches.

15 When the quilting is complete, square up your quilt to 26½ inches (67.3 cm) square.

BINDING

16 Use the method of binding you prefer. This quilt was made with a bias-double-fold binding for strength and sturdiness. To make this binding, first cut bias strips 3½ inches (8.9 cm) wide. You will need about 110 running inches (2.8 m) of bias.

17 Sew the strips together and press the seams open. Fold the bias in half and sew to your quilt, finishing the ends and sewing down using the technique you like best.

attic treasures

DESIGNER

JOAN K. MORRIS

herever the materials for this quilt come from—old tablecloths, worn-out clothing, a vintage store—use them to create a story of time gone by. It's history in the making.

WHAT YOU NEED

Basic Quilting Tool Kit (page 3)

18-inch (45.7 cm) square piece of scrap paper

Scraps of your favorite fabrics (cotton prints, wool, flannel)

White sewing thread

Quilt batting, 18 inches (45.7 cm) square

Muslin fabric, 19 inches (48.3 cm) square

Invisible thread

Scraps of old linens (embroidered or printed)

Assorted lace pieces and ribbons

18 inches (45.7 cm) of ⅜-inch (9.5 mm) wide green velvet ribbon

Embroidery needle (with a large enough eye for embroidery floss, but small enough to pass through size E beads)

Red and black embroidery floss

100 white beads, size E

Beading needle

100 pearl seed beads

15 red glass beads, size E

Assorted buttons

Red ticking fabric, 18 inches (45.7 cm) square

½ yard (45.7 cm) cotton print fabric for the edge

SEAM ALLOWANCE

¼ inch (6 mm)

FINISHED SIZE

19 x 18½ inches (48.3 x 47 cm)

WHAT YOU DO

1 Use the 18-inch (45.7 cm) square of scrap paper as a guide for laying out your scraps of fabric. Play around with placement, size, shape, and color. You want to combine several small pieces into larger rows or blocks of fabric for easier joining later (figure 1).

figure 1

2 With the white thread, sew your pieces together in rows and blocks. Press all seams open. Don't worry if the blocks aren't perfectly square or rectangular. Join all the rows and blocks into a large square. Don't worry about the size, as you will cut it down to an 18-inch (45.7 cm) square later.

3 Center the square of batting under the sewn quilt top. Center the square of muslin under the batting. Pin all three layers in place.

4 Using invisible thread in the top of the machine and white thread in the bobbin, stitch from the top on each seam line ("stitch in the ditch") and around the whole edge of the piece. Start in the center and work your way to the edge to keep the muslin flat underneath.

5 Begin quilting each section of fabric by following the design pattern on the fabric, stitching around shapes, or following stripes or checks. Make each section different, with stitching rows anywhere from ¼ inch to ¾ inch (6 mm to 1.9 cm) apart.

6 Stitch on the lace and ribbon pieces with a straight stitch along all edges. Stitch on any cut-out embroidered pieces using a small zigzag stitch around the whole edge to stop any fraying.

7 Use the embroidery needle and floss to stitch on the blanket stitch, the "x" stitch, and the beaded stitch (using the white beads) along some of the seam lines, and also to embellish the lace with a small stitch.

8 Use the beading needle and white thread to attach the small pearl seed beads. Use the invisible thread to attach the red size E beads and the buttons. When

placing the beads and buttons, be sure to keep them 1 inch (2.5 cm) in from the edge so you can sew on the backing and edge pieces without breaking your machine needle on the beads.

9 Once you have placed all the embellishments, center the square of red ticking fabric on the back of the quilt, right side out, and pin in place.

10 Machine-stitch all the way around the edge, ½ inch (1.3 cm) in from the edge of the red ticking fabric. Trim the quilted piece to match the red ticking fabric backing all the way around the edge.

TURN, TURN, TURN

To quilt the pieces together for the top, you'll have to do a lot of lifting of the presser foot and turning of the piece. Just roll up the excess so it fits in the sewing machine.

11 Cut two pieces of the cotton edge fabric, each 5 x 18 inches (12.7 x 45.7 cm), and two more, each 5 x 20 inches (12.7 x 50.8 cm).

12 Along one of the side edges of the quilt, place one of the 5 x 18-inch (12.7 x 45.7 cm) pieces right sides together with the quilt and stitch ½ inch (1.3 cm) in from the edge. Press the piece to the back of the quilt, creating a ½-inch (1.3 cm) edge on the front. Fold the edge piece in half to the inside and press flat, creating a 2-inch (5.1 cm) back edge. Pin in place. Repeat along the other side edge.

13 For the bottom edge, center one of the 5 x 20-inch (12.7 x 50.8 cm) pieces right sides together and stitch ½ inch (1.3 cm) in from the edge.

Fold the sides in first to cover the side edges and then fold the whole thing to the back and press. Fold the edge piece in half to the inside and press and pin in place.

14 On the top edge, to create a pocket for hanging the piece, center the other 5 x 20-inch (12.7 x 50.8 cm) edge piece right sides together and stitch ½ inch (1.3 cm) in from the edge. Fold and press the sides in, and then the long edge in half to the inside, but this time machine-stitch the side edge in place so there is only one hole for the pocket. Pin in place.

15 With white thread, hand-stitch the whole edge piece to the back, leaving the top side edge open for the pocket.

template

Square Deal, page 31
(enlarge 400%)

	2	
6		5
	1	
7	3	4

about the designers

CINDY COOKSEY has had quilts published in the magazines *Quilters Newsletter* and *Quilts Japan* and in the books *Quilt Visions 2002*, *Portfolio 14 and 15*, and *Embellished Mini-Quilts* (Lark Books, 2007). See her work at www.cindycooksey.com and www.cookseyville.blogspot.com.

KATHY DANIELS has shown her work at sidewalk art festivals, gift shops, and small gallery shows. She also writes and shares her works in progress at her blog www.studiointhewoods. blogspot.com.

MALKA DUBRAWSKY'S work has been in such publications as the *Quilt National* series, *Quilts Baby!*, and *Quilting Arts*. She is the author of *Color Your Cloth: A Quilter's Guide to Dyeing and Patterning Fabric and Fresh Quilting: Fearless Color, Design, and Inspiration*. See her quilts, pillows, and other sundries at www.stitchindye.etsy.com.

JAMIE FINGAL is the author of *Embellished Mini-Quilts*, and she was a featured guest on the PBS show Quilting Arts TV. Learn more about her work at www.jamiefingaldesigns.com and on her Twisted Sister blog at jamiefingaldesigns.blogspot.com.

MARY HUBBARD lives in Maryland with her husband, two sons, and two daughters. See her work at www.whitecloverstitches.etsy. com as well as on www.flickr.com/ whitecloverstitches.

REBEKA LAMBERT has contributed to other Lark Books, including *Pretty Little Potholders*, *Pretty Little Patchwork*, and *Pretty Little Purses & Pouches*. She has a blog at www.artsycraftybabe.typepad. com and an online shop at www. artsycraftybabe.etsy.com.

JOAN K. MORRIS has contributed projects to many publications from Lark Books, including *50 Nifty Beaded Cards*, *Extreme Office Crafts*, *Cutting-Edge Decoupage*, *Pretty Little Pincushions*, *Button! Button!*, and *Pretty Little Potholders*.

AIMEE RAY crafts constantly. She always has a string of projects in the works and many more in mind. Aimee is the author of *Doodle Stitching* and *Doodle Stitching, The Motif Collection*, and she's contributed to many other Lark Books titles. See her work at www.dreamfollow.com.

DORIE BLAISDELL SCHWARZ lives in a small town in Illinois with her husband and daughter. She has contributed to several publications including *Sew Hip* magazine, *Quilts Baby!*, and several titles in the *Pretty Little* series. She keeps a craft blog on the website www.tumblingblocks.net.

RUTH SINGER is a British textile designer-maker who works with organic, sustainable, and upcycled fabrics to create fashion and interior accessories for publications such as *Elle Decoration*, as well as for private commissions. Her work has been exhibited widely. She's written two books: *The Sewing Bible* and *Sew Eco*.

SARAH ANN SMITH is the author of *ThreadWork Unraveled*, a book about using thread on your sewing machine for appliqué, decorative stitching, and quilting.

Sarah writes, teaches, and exhibits her art quilts across the US and internationally, as well as on her website www.sarahannsmith.com.

SUSAN LEWIS STOREY is an award-winning artist in a variety of media. Her art-quilts, digital, and traditional paintings have been featured in various books and magazines for the past ten years. Check out her online portfolio at www.susanstorey.com and her blog at www.susanlewisstorey.com.

JOAN HAND STROH is just a gal who likes to sew. She's been at it since childhood, when her mother let her loose with a huge pair of scissors and a piece of fabric. Lately, she's been sewing and selling retro-inspired aprons. She lives in Texas with her husband, who patiently accompanies her on her endless searches for new fabrics. See more of her work at momomadeit.etsy.com.

Others in the Simply Series

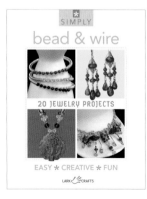

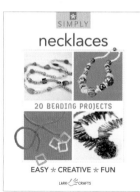